GIOVANNI GABRIELI

IN ECCLESIIS

Motet for soloists, chorus,
instruments and organ continuo

edited by

DENIS STEVENS

Order No: NOV 030757

NOVELLO PUBLISHING LIMITED

PREFACE

In ecclesiis, first published in Giovanni Gabrieli's *Symphoniae Sacrae II* (1615), and printed for the first time in score in Carl von Winterfield's *Johannes Gabrieli und sein Zeitalter* (1834), may be ranked among the master's best-known motets. It is indeed a work of remarkable proportions and sonority, intended no doubt for one of the many splendid occasions of state when the Doge in person and the Venetian Signory attended the basilica of San Marco or some other great church of the island city.

Unfortunately for Gabrieli, the essence of his composition has not generally been transmitted to the world of musical performance with the degree of accuracy in transcription and liveliness in realization that such a masterpiece demands. The original organ part remained for a long time unknown, and the disposition of the eight vocal lines remained for the most part unclear, so that the composer's carefully-wrought symmetry of tonal architecture has been set askew.

The polychoral works of Giovanni and of his uncle Andrea Gabrieli are distinguished by a strong propensity for choirs of dissimilar range and vocal content. Yet in spite of this obvious feature, *In ecclesiis* is usually presented as a double-choir motet for two equal groups of SATB. That nothing could be further from the musical truth is shown by the following table of ranges, to which the original nomenclature of the part-books has been added:

The two groups obviously require S A T T / A T Bar. B, or (if tenors are in short supply), S A T Bar. / A T Bar. B. It is also clear from the texture of the music written for the first group that Gabrieli had soloists in mind, not only because of the various solos and duets occurring between bars 1 and 173, but also in view of the virtuosic nature of the peroration, from bar 205 to 213 especially. Bar 213 reveals the true position of the two lower voices in the solo group, for although *Octavus* and *Tenor* are almost identical in range, the cadence confirms the range-chart by giving the root of the chord to the *Tenor* (assigned to T or Bar. in the present edition). As a purely practical measure, and in order not to exclude sopranos from modern performances, I have suggested mixing sopranos and altos on the top line of the main choir. In this way, everyone will have something to sing, and the four parts should blend and balance satisfactorily.

Problems of balance inevitably occur when modern brass instruments are substituted for the composer's cornetti and trombones, which in his day and age had a relatively soft and soothing tone — a perfect polyphonic back-cloth for the duet from bar 68 to 112. One possible solution is to use three oboes, tenor trombone I or viola (Gabrieli says Violino, meaning a member of the violin family as opposed to the viols, and implying a tenor violin by range), tenor trombone II and bass trombone. This makes a perfectly acceptable 'broken consort', and the only adjustments required (due to the compass of oboe III) are a brief exchange of parts — oboe III and trombone I or viola — from bar 56 to 58; and an alternative for the low A in bar 207. These adjustments have been incorporated into the present score, but if conductors prefer to use a trumpet or a cor anglais for the third line (oboe III), the few notes concerned can easily be restored as they were.

In San Marco, composers made extensive use of the galleries and of a smaller gallery for musicians called the *palco*, nearer the floor level of the basilica. Canaletto, in one of his rare Venetian interiors, immortalized it in a drawing which delineates its function with considerable clarity. It is reproduced in François Lesure's *Music and Art in Society*, published by the Pennsylvania State University Press. These galleries suited to perfection the performance lay-out for such a motet as *In ecclesiis*, since each group — vocal soloists, choir (doubled by instruments according to the classical meaning of *a capella*), and instrumental consort — would occupy a different level or position from the point of view of a member of the congregation, no matter where he sat. Each group would have its own continuo instrument; and if this seems a luxury today, it should nevertheless be budgeted for when conductors are able to aim at this particular kind of spatial separation. The organ continuo given in the present score can be used effectively by portative, positive, or other small organs, and even by plucked-string instruments, which however are not to be strongly recommended.

The realization of the continuo, the interpretation of the *musica ficta*, the marks of speed and dynamics, and in certain cases the text-underlay, are all editorial. Readers will notice that I do not recommend the sharp to middle C in the SA line of the chorus at *Alleluia* (bar 16 and subsequently); and I hope that they will accept my advocacy of Gabrieli's doubtless intentional false-relations at bars 72, 75 and 80. The cadence at bar 111, for the two uppermost instrumental parts, is not made absolutely clear in the part-books, but I think that here again a false-relation is intended.

Although the Latin text is non-liturgical, yet appropriate for a solemn occasion in which church and state (as so often in Venice) joined hands in prayer, certain echoes can be found in missals and breviaries. An offertory *In ecclesiis benedicite* occurs in Carolus Ott's *Offertoriale sive versus offertoriorum cantus Gregoriani* (Desclée, 1935). A short antiphon *In ecclesiis benedicite Domino* follows the psalm *Exsurgat Deus* (Feria quarta ad Laudes), in which this very phrase may be found; and there is also a responsory beginning *In ecclesiis benedicite Deo* (Feria secunda) sung in the fourth week after Easter. Gabrieli's text does not agree with these in its subsequent ramifications, but the importance he obviously attached to the oft-repeated Alleluias indicates that a feast not far from Easter may well have been the *raison d'être* for the motet. It will be noticed that the first half of the text stresses the singular (*mea, meo, meum*) and the second half the plural (*noster, nos*), perhaps reflecting the Doge and his subjects intent on celebrating some major feast in the Venetian calendar. In a year in which Easter Sunday fell on April 2, Monday (Feria secunda) of the fourth week would be April 21, or St Mark's Day.

I should like to express my sincere thanks to Mr Desmond Ratcliffe and Mr Michael Riches for their expert assistance in preparing this work for the press.

DENIS STEVENS
Geneva
December 1970

Instrumental parts are available on hire.

In ecclesiis benedicite Domino, Alleluia.

In omni loco dominationis benedic anima mea Dominum, Alleluia.

In Deo salutari meo et gloria mea,

       Deus auxilium meum et spes mea in Deo est, Alleluia.

Deus noster, te invocamus, te laudamus, te adoramus;

       libera nos, salva nos, vivifica nos, Alleluia.

Deus adiutor noster in aeternum, Alleluia.

In the congregations, bless ye the Lord, Alleluia.

In every place of the dominion bless, O my soul, the Lord, Alleluia.

In God my salvation and my glory;

       God is my help and my hope is in God, Alleluia.

Our God, we invoke thee, we praise thee, we worship thee;

       free us, keep us safe, grant us life, Alleluia.

God our helper in eternity, Alleluia.

IN ECCLESIIS

Edited by Denis Stevens

GIOVANNI GABRIELI

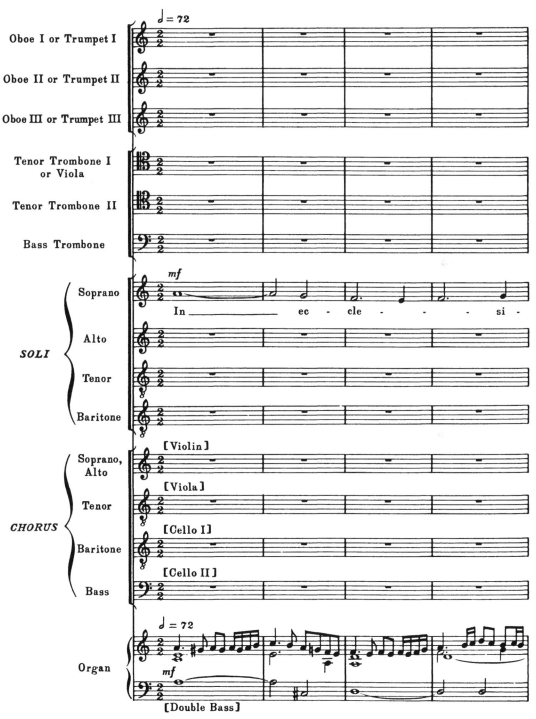

4

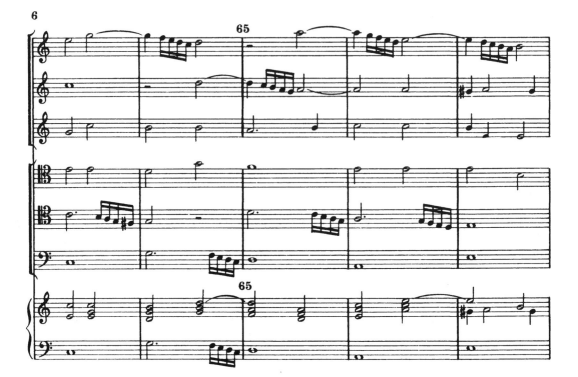

me - - - - - um et spes me - a in De - o

- - - um et spes me - a

est, in De - o est, et spes me - a

in De - o est, in De - o est, et spes

16

19937